# of Stone

Hearts of Flesh

A Positive Approach to the Ten Commandments

Fr. Thomas G. Caserta

Pauline
BOOKS & MEDIA
BOSTON

Nihil Obstat:
Rev. Richard J. Malone, S.T.L., Th.D.

Imprimatur:
†Bernard Cardinal Law

August 29, 1995

Library of Congress Cataloging-in-Publication Data

Caserta, Thomas G., 1952-
Tablets of stone, hearts of flesh / Thomas G. Caserta.
p. cm.
ISBN 0-8198-7387-X
1. Ten commandments—Devotional use. 2. spiritual life—Catholic Church. 3. Catholic Church—Doctrines. I. Title.
BV4655.C27 1996
241.5'2—dc20 95-41901
CIP

Cover design: Helen Rita Lane, FSP

Printed and published by Pauline Books & Media, 50 St. Paul's Avenue, Boston, MA 02130.

Pauline Books & Media is the publishing house of the Daughters of St. Paul, an international congregation of women religious serving the Church with the communications media.

1 2 3 4 99 98 97 96

To the staff and seminarians,
both past and present,
of Cathedral Residence,
Douglaston, New York.

Contents

Introduction

Can you imagine what the world would be like if everyone followed the Ten Commandments? Crime would melt away. Women wouldn't be afraid to walk alone at night. People wouldn't have to lock their doors. Families would live together in peace. Everyone could be trusted to tell the truth.

It sounds utopian, doesn't it? But the Ten Commandments provide a prescription for peaceful living. At first when someone suggested to me that I write a series of spiritual reflections on the Ten Commandments, I dismissed the idea immediately. All those "thou shalt nots" can seem so negative. Isn't it better to stress the positive? But then I realized that the Ten Commandments actually do contain a positive focus. It's true that the negative wording forbids certain actions. But they aim at positive results. We need to focus on the implicit positive behavior suggested by the explicit prohibition. In this light, the following reflections were born.

The Book of Exodus recounts how God delivered the Israelites from slavery in Egypt and formed them into a people of his own. God entered into a covenant with them and gave them a law to observe. Exodus narrates that Moses climbed down from the mountain of God carrying the stone tablets of the law. Later in the Old Testament, many prophets declared to the chosen people that God would transform their hearts into hearts of flesh. "And I will give them one heart, and put a new spirit within them; I will take the stony heart out of their flesh and give them a heart of flesh" (Ez 11:19). The law of God is not only concerned with external behavior. Its primary purpose is to inflame our hearts with a love that burns for God. In a sense, the tablets of stone were to be inscribed in the flesh-and-blood hearts of God's people. This enabled them to affirm with the psalmist: "He only is my rock and my salvation, my fortress; I shall not be shaken" (Ps 62:6). When the law is inscribed upon the heart, we can see that the commandments do not call us to merely comply with external rules. They express the deepest dictates of our created being, our longing for God.

It is impossible to divorce the meaning of the Ten Commandments from the overall meaning of the Exodus event. If we are to appreciate the impact of the commandments on our lives, we must grasp how the Exodus event etched itself into Israel's consciousness. The Exodus engendered Israel's great intimacy with God. For so many other nations their gods were a little like ghosts. They were mysterious and usually indifferent to the situations of mortals. The God of Israel was different. He revealed himself as a God who would abide with his people to save them. He declared to Moses: "I have seen the affliction of my people who are in Egypt, and have heard their cry because of their taskmasters; I know their sufferings" (Ex 3:7). The Israelites' misery stirred God to intervene. He promised to act on their behalf, and his action outstripped their wildest expectations. God liberated Israel from slavery and led them into their own land where they were free to be a people God cherished. The Lord sealed his promise of deliverance with mighty acts of salvation. He became for Israel the *suzerain* or guarantor of a covenant which would endure for all time. In turn, Israel was to be faithful to her Lord who protects and delivers her.

The Ten Commandments are signposts. They point out the way by which those who are in a covenant with God journey toward full union with him. They do not merely regulate external behavior. They give voice to the way a heart which longs for God desires to live. By forbidding certain behavior, the tablets of stone invite us to a life based on an intimate experience of God who abides with and saves us.

Dietrich Bonhoeffer once wrote that "cheap grace" does not exist. A life in God exacts a high price. Moses and Israel suffered much for it. It cost Jesus his blood as he agonized on the cross. It will cost us, too. Our fidelity to God demands sacrifice. These meditations can remind us of what God's covenant demands of us. God has redeemed us. In the secret of our hearts, we all know how God snatched us from the muck we wallowed in. It is not enough to shout "Praise God!" I must live in a way which radiates that God holds first place in my life. Our society glamorizes power, fashion, sex, money and fame. Though not evil in themselves, they cannot set the standards by which I live my life. I must begin to see how they pale in comparison with the compassion, love, gentleness and fidelity which mark the lives of those redeemed in Christ.

In the Book of Deuteronomy we read: "For this commandment which I command you this day is not too hard for you, neither is it far off.... But the word is very near you; it is in your mouth and in your heart, so that you can do it" (Deut 30:11, 14). This instruction from Deuteronomy can lead us beyond the apparent negativity of the Ten Commandments. The wisdom of God which hovers over the Scriptures will enlighten us to treasure this tenfold invitation to a life in union with the God we long for. Openness to this wisdom will enable us to see that the tablets of Sinai are congruent with the contours of our hearts. Such a vision induces a conversion which can renew God's "ancient Church in ageless youth."

Letting Go of Our Idols

The evening before I was ordained to the priesthood, I conversed with an older priest whose wisdom I greatly respected. He stunned me when he said, "You will meet priests who do not believe in God." I thought that was harsh and absurd. How could a man who had given his life to God and the Church not believe in those very realities? My friend continued, "You will meet men who believe in canon law, psychology, dogmatic theology, pastoral counseling, and finance, but somehow God doesn't enter the picture."

The sixteen years of my priesthood have marshaled evidence which bears this out. I have found that Christians too quickly forget the radical demand of the First Commandment: "I am the Lord your God...you shall have no other gods before me" (Ex 20:2). If we are to understand the positive dimension of the First Commandment we must be honest enough to face the reality of idolatry in our lives. Few of us sacrifice to stone statues or bow down before golden calves. Our idols are more subtle. We may fear that our world will cave in if we break free of their hold on us.

We live in a society which values appearance over reality. We must look good at all costs. We idolize our reputation.

In order to maintain it we will lie and cover up our mistakes. We shrink from admitting failure or error. We have turned excuses, equivocations and rationalizations into a fine art of self-preservation. Have we not enshrined our reputation as a god? It is certainly virtuous to preserve our good name. But only people who are grounded in God's unconditional love can admit and grow from mistakes and failure. They do not need to prop themselves up with false supports. They know that they are more than their reputation or attributes. Their concern is to root themselves in God and not to grasp at a reputation or name which floats on the shifting currents of human opinion, like a branch bobbing down the rapids of a river.

Just as we can idolize our reputation or image, we can also make a god of our point of view or way of doing things. We often act as if we believe the popular jibe: "There are two ways of doing things: my way and the wrong way." We can become so wedded to our point of view, our field of expertise, our "way," that this concern eclipses God. Those involved in church leadership may fall into this trap. Many of us were educated and earned degrees in valuable fields like pastoral counseling, spirituality, theology or education. But we must be wary of absolutizing these fields into ends in themselves so that we lose sight of God. The Christian worships God alone. To the extent that counseling and theology draw us closer to God and make us more aware of his covenant with us, they achieve their purpose. When they become ends in themselves and distract us from the divine wisdom they are meant to serve, they may hinder our relationship with God. We must learn that in spite of psychology's potential, theology's wisdom or canon law's clarity, there is no other God but the Lord.

What word best captures the spirit of this commandment? It is *abandonment.* Abandonment highlights the positive aspect of the First Commandment. By prohibiting idolatry, God invites us to abandon all we have and are into his wise and loving hands. The abandoned heart knows that God is more powerful than any of its own efforts. Abandonment reassures me that, even if my whole life collapses into failure like a shack in an earthquake, God can still draw forth infinite beauty and goodness from the ruins. The world is still in God's hands, not in ours. Abandonment urges us not to abdicate our responsibility but to anchor our efforts in his love. In this way no created reality can lure our hearts away from our Lord and God.

This abandonment is the foundation of genuine sanctity. One of the great paradoxes of the spiritual life is that although holiness requires our efforts, it is totally God's work. We become holy when we no longer make sanctity an end in itself but allow God himself to be our sanctity.

A story by J. F. Powers illustrates this point. It tells of a young priest who had desired contemplative holiness from his seminary days. But through daily contact with parish life and a saintly pastor he discovers that great holiness is not so much to drown in the sea of God but to float into shore and bask in the warm sand between your toes. As Teresa of Avila pointed out four centuries ago, sanctity is not a matter of thinking much or doing much but of loving much. The First Commandment calls us to a life in which God holds the central place. This commandment invites us to allow God's gentle power to shatter the idols and illusions of our hearts so that we can see how blessed are those who open themselves to what God has to give.

For Personal Reflection

1. What have I substituted for God in my life?

2. Are there any personal relationships in my life which are keeping me from being all that God has created me to be?

3. Do I ever lie or manipulate others simply to preserve my reputation?

4. What specific step can I take *now* to abandon myself more completely into God's hands?

Notes

Prayer

Christ,
enlighten the darkness of my mind and heart.
Send your Spirit of truth powerfully
into my life so that I may see the idols
that my fear and blindness have created.
Give me the courage to shatter
these false gods and abandon myself
ever more fully into the loving hands
of our heavenly Father, the only true God
who with you and the Holy Spirit
lives and reigns forever and ever.

Amen.

Reverence: Caring for the Sacred

A friend of mine tells how he found a letter his father wrote to his mother over fifty years ago. While the contents of the letter can touch the reader's heart, even more impressive is the way his mother treasured it for over half a century. Although crinkled and yellowed with age, it spoke of love. Human beings have a need to guard and protect the realities which they cherish. We call this care *reverence.* We are vigilant for those persons and things which we clasp to our hearts. This care for what we hold sacred is the foundation of reverence.

Ancient Israel's experience was the same. Israel prized the redeeming presence of God as her most precious possession. That presence was expressed in God's very name. So great was Israel's determination to guard the sacred character of God's presence that his name was never even pronounced, let alone called to witness something false or unholy. The Second Commandment prohibited any form of blasphemy or disrespect for the holiness of God's name. That name expressed God's covenant relationship with his people.

Traditionally we have viewed the Second Commandment as forbidding all unnecessary swearing, foul language and irreverent use of the name of God or Jesus. The commandment certainly involves these aspects. But we can discover a richer level of meaning. The Second Commandment calls us to care for the sacred. It invites us to a life of reverence.

If we are to understand what a life of reverence means, we must first appreciate what some philosophers and theologians have called the sacramental nature of reality. This means that we view created matter as a way to encounter the perfection of the Creator, and see finite reality as an avenue which leads to the infinite. As a poet phrased it, this means "to see heaven in a grain of sand and eternity in an hour." At times the pressures in our lives can eclipse this attitude of reverence. The Second Commandment reminds us to break free of these superficial pressures and cynicism and open our eyes to the sacred which surrounds us.

We can strive to retrieve our sense of reverence in three areas especially: our relationship with God, our appreciation of others and our respect for sacred objects.

The Catholic community has nourished devotion to the name of Jesus. Our rich tradition has always esteemed the holy name of God's Son. However there is more behind devotion to the name of God than we might first perceive. It means more than simply not taking God's name in vain. Our God, through his Son, Jesus the Lord, has called us into a loving relationship with himself. This gentle invitation presents itself in every area of our lives. Reverence means being able to identify and cherish the many faces of God's invitation to this union.

We can become so casual about God's love for us! Yet that love is a force which sustains us in being and rejuvenates us. God is the Lord of heaven and earth, the Creator of the stars and sky, and the one who commands the winds and the seas. Yet God in his tenderness desires to make his home in us to love us. The love of another finite human being can often change the course of our lives. How much more can the love of God poured out in his Son transform us! No wonder that St. Paul can cry out that anyone who believes in Christ is a new creation (cf. 2 Cor 5:17). The Second Commandment does not merely prohibit blasphemy. It calls us to venerate and esteem the name of God who cares for us. Such reverence not only invites us to honor God's name in speech, but also to appreciate his presence in every aspect of life, even to the end of the world (cf. Mt 28:20).

Closely related to our relationship with God is an awareness of the sacredness of our relationships with others. At times we may think that our interpersonal relationships have little bearing on our spiritual lives. But our tradition has valued these bonds as a road to God. Great writers like Aelred of Rievaulx, Richard of St. Victor and Teresa of Avila emphasized the importance of sound personal friendships for spiritual growth. We need to recover a sense of reverence for the presence of God in other persons. Our life with others must go deeper than what pop psychology recommends. "Deep calls to deep" (Ps 42:7). If we are to live in reverence for one another, we must respect the mystery of "God-living-in-us" as it encounters the mystery of "God-living-within-another." We must acknowledge the dignity of other persons because they are made in the image and likeness of God just as we are. The Jesuit poet Gerard Manley Hopkins powerfully captured our need to reverence the presence of God in others when he observed: "Christ plays in ten thousand places, lovely in limbs, and lovely in eyes not his, to the Father through the features of men's faces." When we struggle for that kind of vision in our dealings with others, we achieve reverential care for those whom the Father has given us to love.

Our final area of reverence is to guard the integrity of sacred objects, which might appear outmoded for our time. Aren't we more concerned with the meaning behind sacred objects and events than with the objects themselves? If we focus on objects, aren't we in danger of slipping into the realm of the magical or superstitious?

Here again we must emphasize the sacramental nature of reality. We certainly never honor an object for its own sake. But we do recognize its ability to mediate or facilitate an encounter with the sacred. The sacred images and books in our homes may become so familiar to us that we need to challenge ourselves to recall the deeper meaning which they mediate. The danger of going to magical or superstitious extremes in this matter can arise. To avoid this, we should realize that a religious article is not a charm. It would be a contradiction to wear a religious medal while acting in an unchristian way, or to display a sacred image in the home and still engage in the backbiting and petty bitterness that so often tears families apart. Caring for sacred objects can make us more aware of how fully the sacred realities they represent engulf our lives. We are "surrounded by so great a cloud of witnesses" (Heb 12:1) which can continually motivate us to keep "looking to Jesus the pioneer and perfecter of our faith" (Heb 12:2).

The Second Commandment reminds us of the necessity for reverence in our lives. An ancient oriental story teaches us a great lesson. An old king had a daughter whose beauty delighted all who saw her. But she refused to marry. The king had resigned himself to dying without seeing her wed. One day she made a drum of pure silk and told him she would marry any man who could hear the drum's sound. More distraught than ever, the old king cried that no one can hear the sound of a silk drum. Some time later a handsome prince from a faraway land came to ask for his daughter's hand. "Surely," the old man exclaimed, "you cannot have heard the sound of the silken drum." The young man replied: "No, I have come because I heard its silence."

When we are able to hear the silent melody of life, to see the dancing in the stillness and the sacred in the common clay of daily life, we will have learned to live God's Second Commandment.

For Personal Reflection

1. Do I have a sense of loving reverence for the deeper meaning of life? Am I able to find God "beneath the surface" of things?

2. Do I have a loving care for the name of Jesus? Am I as aware as I should be of the power and the prayer available to me in the holy name?

3. Do I have a sense of loving reverence for the people in my life, especially family and friends, whose love is so important for my spiritual growth?

4. In what concrete ways can I be more reverent toward God and other persons in my life?

Notes

Prayer

God, Creator of all things, giver of all life,
help me to see your divine presence in every
moment and every situation of my life.
Fill me with a spirit of loving reverence
for you and all your creation.
Help me to see your hand in whatever life
may bring. Give me the wisdom to honor
the people you send into my life
as special bearers of your presence.
Above all, increase my faith in your Son,
our Lord Jesus Christ, so that I may recognize
the power and prayer available to me in his
holy name.

Amen.

The Gift of Rest

In a remarkable poem entitled *The Pulley,* the great seventeenth-century poet George Herbert depicts God pouring out all his blessings on humanity. As he comes to the end of the glass out of which he is lavishing his bounty, God notices that *rest* is the last of the blessings. He decides to withhold this blessing from his creatures. In the poem God says:

> For if I should (said he)
> Bestow this jewel also on my creature,
> He would adore my gifts instead of me,
> And rest in nature, not the God of nature:
> So both should losers be.

God's reason for this provides a rich source of meditation on the Third Commandment: "You shall keep holy the sabbath day." In withholding rest, or a sense of satisfaction, God is insuring that we will find our complete fulfillment and rest only in God, and not in any created reality.

Our Christian tradition recognizes the sabbath or the Lord's day as Sunday. It is no accident that we call it the day of rest. We need a weekly reminder that this world is not our permanent home, despite its beauty and grandeur. The Lord's day helps us to recall that we have our citizenship in heaven, as St. Paul wrote to the Philippians (cf. Phil 3:20). Sunday is meant to remind us that we belong primarily to the Lord, even amid all the rush and responsibility that comprise our lives. God alone can fulfill us and slake our thirst for peace.

Someone once said that Christians can become so caught up in the works of God that they can forget the God of works. Herbert's poem underlines this point, which is the message of the sabbath day. One day a week we need time and a change of routine to remember that the Lord directs our lives and that he is the God of creation.

Christian adoration thrives on this attitude. Adoration implies the ability to step out of myself, to empty myself of my own cares and concerns, and focus on the greatness of God simply because he is the Good in my life. By its very nature adoration requires that I put aside the ordinary details of life and rivet my attention on the God who has given all to me. It leads us to echo the sentiments of the psalmist: "For God alone my soul waits in silence; from him comes my salvation" (Ps 62:1).

This understanding of the Third Commandment is far more profound than to see it simply as an obligation to attend Mass, which binds under pain of sin. While certainly the Sunday Mass precept obliges every Catholic, our motivation can be so much richer than merely to keep a law. We observe the sabbath to honor the Creator who is infinitely greater than the creature.

The Third Commandment questions us: "Do we take time for God?" It challenges us to examine the priority we place on spending time with God. How much time are we willing to spend with God not only once a week, but every day? One of the "sins" of good people is that we have time for everyone else and none for ourselves. We do not place a high priority on taking time to be alone with ourselves and with God. It is no wonder that so often we feel empty. As Herbert says, we begin to adore the gifts and not the Giver. We attempt to rest in created reality and not in the one who alone is Real.

The Third Commandment invites us to go beyond our busyness and activity to a deeper and more centered life. As Henri Nouwen has pointed out, this life is one which can convert the frenetic and often lonely sense of our preoccupied activity into an experience of solitude where I can be present to myself and to my God. This is the ultimate sabbath observance: when I can see every day as the Lord's and when I can put aside the many burdens of life to adore the Lord who has said, "Come to me, all who labor and are heavy laden, and I will give you rest" (Mt 11:28).

A contemporary hymn speaks of this: "Like a shepherd he feeds his flock and gathers the lambs in his arms, holding them carefully close to his heart, leading them home." In the rush and routine of our week we need a day when we can pause and experience the shepherd's embrace and open our hearts to his gentle leading. The commandment of sabbath rest bids us to experience the holiness of God. It can mean simply a leisurely walk or drive to church and a quiet day with family, friends or even a good book. God has freely chosen to place a spark of that holiness into our hearts. The quiet and rest of our sabbath observance will fan that spark into a flame which will renew the face of the earth.

For Personal Reflection

1. Do I try to make God a part of each day of my life? Do I truly try to give him first place?

2. To the best of my ability do I try to keep Sunday as a day of sabbath rest? Do I try to make Sunday a day of leisure and joy?

3. Do I understand the richness of adoration for my spiritual life? Do I make wonder and awe at the goodness of God a regular part of my prayer?

4. What specific thing can I do to make next Sunday more of a sabbath of rest for me and my family?

Notes

Prayer

Lord Jesus Christ, you said,
"Come to me all you who are weary and
find life burdensome and I will give you rest."
I turn to you now with all my cares
and heartaches, all my joys and plans.
Help me to see that my heart will only know
rest when I rest in you who are perfect peace.
Quiet my longings, calm my fears and fill me
with the joy that comes from you alone.
Renew in me every day, but especially
every Sunday, an awareness of your presence
in my life.
Help my life to be a clear witness that
to know you is to live and to serve you
is the only wisdom.

Amen.

Home and Hospitality

How would you describe the love your parents had for you? When someone recently asked me that question, I realized that although I am very aware of how much my parents loved me, it was difficult for me to isolate one way in which they showed that love. After some thought, I had to say that they best expressed their love and support by allowing me to be my own person. Their affection called me forth and challenged me to be the self I really was. They accepted that self even when it may not have conformed to what they had planned for me. They loved *me* more than their dreams for me.

That question drew me to reflect on the meaning of the Fourth Commandment: "Honor your father and mother" (Ex 20:12). Christians often misunderstand the responsibilities which they bear toward their parents and toward their children. Sometimes our homes resemble army camps as parents scream at their children like a drill sergeant. At other times children may yell at their parents. Other homes are more like hotels, whose occupants barely have time to nod "hello" to each other as they rush out to work and school. Christian families today need to make special efforts to transform their home life into a haven where both parents and children can find love and support.

One contemporary writer suggests that the ancient virtue of hospitality offers a means to achieve this goal. At first it might seem strange to talk of showing hospitality to our own parents and children. They are so close to us, and we may associate hospitality with strangers. A deeper look will reveal a different reality. Henri Nouwen has described hospitality as the virtue by which we create a free and friendly space in which our guests can be themselves, be refreshed and then move on in their journey. We can apply that insight to our family life. Hospitality in the family means learning to love each other and learning to let go.

So often we want to hold on to those we love. This is a natural instinct. Only a mature and creative love can allow the beloved the freedom and support to forge their own way and to carve their own future. Anyone who has tried to cling to a loved one in a way that limits freedom can speak of the sometimes tragic results.

Children may sometimes think that "honoring Mom and Dad" means doing whatever they say. Parents, too, may assume that the only way their children can show them honor and respect is for the children to do exactly what the parents command. I would suggest that both parents and children can best observe the Fourth Commandment by giving each other the freedom to be their own selves. As a child grows up, he or she eventually needs to let go of the infantile notion that Mom and Dad can make all of the hurts go away, that they have all the answers. This does not make parents any less deserving of love and respect. Instead, children may grow to esteem their parents even more when they see them as human beings who struggle to love as best they can, often despite insurmountable odds. A realization dawns that Mom and Dad are imperfect people. This in turn leads to that understanding and love which builds up the Christian home.

On the other hand, parents need to let go of the idea that their success or failure as persons depends on how their children turn out. Because a son or daughter encounters difficulty or failure, does not mean that the parents are to blame. To gauge one's self-worth by the accomplishments of one's offspring is to burden both the children and oneself. Perhaps Mom and Dad need to let go of their need to be perfect parents. At times parents can forge deeper family bonds if they share some of their struggles and fears with their children in an appropriate way. They should be confident that the children will still love and respect them despite their flaws.

Parents may have God-given authority and responsibility in a family, but this does not make them equal to divinity. God is still the Lord even in the family. God calls Christian parents to move beyond a mere concern for discipline and pass on their faith, their hopes and even their failure to their children. The Lord also calls them to foster a home environment in which children feel free to question and search for their own way and their own convictions. It is especially difficult for parents to allow their children the freedom to fail or be hurt. It may wrench their hearts but they can't rescue their children from every pain and difficulty of life. They can certainly offer love and support. But to over-protect one's children is to cripple their growth.

This is not to deny the need for rules and limits in the Christian home. Genuine love always seeks a structure for its authentic expression. Hospitality in the Christian home means simply that persons are valued over rules and that obedience flows from real love and affection. In bidding us to honor our parents, the Fourth Commandment challenges us to treat our parents as persons who deserve our love and respect, despite their imperfections. It reminds parents, as St. Paul urged, "Do not provoke your children to anger" (Eph 6:4). Such an atmosphere of mutual love will foster a genuinely Christian family life, where both parents and children can find happiness and support.

For Personal Reflection

1. Do I try to see the people in my family as *persons,* with each one's uniqueness, gifts and limitations?

2. Do I try "to create a free and friendly space" in my heart for each member of my family? Who is a special challenge to me in this task?

3. In what specific ways can I show in word and in action the love I have for my family members?

4. Are there issues in my family which need to be addressed so that we can be more loving and Christ-like? What is the best way to accomplish this?

Notes

Prayer

Lord Jesus Christ,
you lived a full and complete family life
with Mary and Jospeh in Nazareth.
Deepen the love and mutual respect
of my family.
If we have wounded each other
through human weakness and sin,
teach us the ways to heal those wounds.
If we are happy and content,
strengthen and increase our love
for one another and for you.
Above all, help us to see in our family life
an image of the perfection
of relationship and love that you share
with your Father and the Holy Spirit
as you live and reign as God forever and ever.

Amen.

Love for Life

When I was a child, a priest in our parish tried to relax people about going to confession by saying, "As long as you haven't killed anyone since breakfast, there's nothing to worry about." From that time on I never thought much about the Fifth Commandment. Since I have never killed anyone, I am safe on that score. But is that all this commandment demands? Although we may at times assume this commandment does not apply to our daily lives, a closer look at it reveals a deeper meaning.

As startling as it may seem, Christians frequently can kill. Our victims are most often ourselves. At times we kill ourselves by not taking care of our physical needs. We can burden ourselves with needless guilt and we can disregard our own value as unique and lovable persons created by God. Certainly this is not the usual sense that comes to mind when we think of killing. But if we pause to consider it, this outlook can foster our spiritual growth.

St. Paul asks: "Do you not know that your body is a temple of the Holy Spirit within you?" (1 Cor 6:19). How often do I desecrate God's temple? I do this when I fill it with junk food, eat too much or too little, abuse it with alcohol or drugs, deprive it of legitimate rest, and neglect physical exercise. Our bodies are precious treasures which God bestowed on us in his love.

Does this mean that having a body which glows with health and beauty equals being a good Christian? Certainly not! But it does mean that we have a moral obligation to care for our physical and emotional wellbeing. No virtue requires that we rush about all day, trying to do so much good that we lack time for a nourishing meal and some quiet relaxation. Such a lifestyle could even reflect a subtle form of pride, which deceives me into thinking that without my efforts the world may not survive.

Another way we Christians frequently kill ourselves is through needless guilt. Some guilt can be good and healthy. If I am responsible for having done something wrong, then my guilt feelings alert me to the need to seek forgiveness. They spur me to repent and to make amends for my wrongdoing.

But an unhealthy guilt can sap my emotional well-being. I may feel guilty about things in which I had no say or very little choice. I may soak in guilt like a sponge over things I am not accountable for. In situations like these I often take other people's mistakes on my shoulders, assume responsibility for their errors and berate myself for sins which I did not commit. This guilt can be a kind of self-crucifixion, a way in which I do indeed "kill" myself. Unfortunately, many times we confuse this guilt with Christian piety. Nothing could be further from the truth. Jesus was already crucified. His death was the perfect sacrifice. We do not have to improve upon it! If I find myself in this situation of needless guilt, consulting with a spiritual director or qualified counselor can assist me in caring for my emotional wellbeing.

The final form of our "killing" sums up the first two ways. We fail to value our unique, God-created self. St. Augustine is credited with saying that God loves each one of us as if we were the only person in the world. St. Paul tells us that we are God's work of art, created in Christ Jesus (cf. Eph 2:10). But we may overlook the beauty God gave us in creating us. So we settle for the casual sexual encounter instead of the abiding and loving commitment, and for the alcohol or drug-induced "high" instead of genuine enthusiasm for life. We are content with half-hearted efforts instead of challenging ourselves to put forth all that we are capable of. Instead we should be like a runner who exerts every effort to win a race as he speeds along the track. Again St. Paul urges us: "Do you not know that in a race all the runners compete, but only one receives the prize? So run that you may obtain it" (1 Cor 9:24).

The Fifth Commandment forbids all activity which harms human life. On the spiritual journey we soon grasp that life is more than brain waves and heartbeats. It is a fire that allows our lives to burn for the greater glory of God. In a story from the *Sayings of The Desert Fathers* a young monk is not satisfied with the ordinary ascetical practices such as fasting, solitude and long vigils of prayer. He asks his spiritual father what more he should do in order to grow in holiness. The older monk raises his hands aloft as sparks seem to shoot out of them. He eyes the young monk and replies: "Why not be turned completely into fire!" A meditation on the Fifth Commandment might help us to catch that spark which will set us aglow and move us forward toward the day when God will be all in all (cf. 1 Cor 15:28).

For Personal Reflection

1. Do I truly value my life as created and loved by God? How can I grow in appreciation of this truth?

2. Do I take the ordinary means to care for my physical health? Do my attitudes toward relaxation, food and exercise, as well as my use of alcohol and drugs, show that I see life as God's greatest gift?

3. Do I have a balanced sense of responsibility for my actions? Do I shoulder needless or uncalled-for guilt? If so, how can I change that pattern in my life?

4. In what specific ways can I live life more enthusiastically as a child of God?

Notes

Prayer

Lord Jesus Christ,
you have revealed yourself as the way,
the truth and the life.
Fill me with a love and reverence
for your precious gift of life.
Guard me from any actions or attitudes
which might harm or lessen my life
or the lives of others.
Enable me to embrace both
the difficulty and the joy of living.
Fill me with the sure hope
that each day lived in integrity and love
brings me closer to you
who are the source and Lord of all life
forever and ever.

Amen.

Paying Attention to Love

In his book *The Seven Capital Sins Today,* Henry Fairlie makes an interesting observation about lust. He points out that lust prevents us from paying attention to the reality of love. Fairlie observes: "This attention needs no less to be given to someone we love. The gaze does not peer, it learns how to look and, learning how to look, learns how to love." The Sixth Commandment insures the integrity and dignity of the expression of sexual love. In the past and perhaps even today, Catholics sometimes overemphasized the "thou shalt not" in regard to sexuality. If we look more closely at this commandment, we find that it urges us to pay attention to love.

Today sex saturates our society. Advertisers use it to entice consumers to buy the latest product. The media use it to allure the unwary, or worse, to corrupt the innocent. Sex fascinates our society, which has severed it from the expression of love for which God intended it. So in dealing with sexuality we focus on pleasure.

In the proper context sexual pleasure is a good. God meant us to enjoy sex or he would have created us otherwise. But if we divorce it from a committed and caring love in marriage, sex quickly degenerates to a lust which leaves us empty and unfulfilled. What a difference exists between having sex and making love. The Sixth Commandment challenges us to insure that sexual experience always expresses a committed and holy marital love.

God invites us to rejoice in sexuality. The "thou shalt not" simply forbids whatever would prevent us from delighting in the experience of sexuality as God intended it to be: a union which seals the love of a husband and wife. Christian tradition has always specified that marriage is the proper context of any sexual relationship. Passions which toss us about on the seas of desire may hinder us from reverencing sexuality. But a Christian awareness of the dignity of sexual union can help us insure that our gaze is never a leer, our touch never a manipulation, and our desires never prurient self-interest.

In the past, some Christians viewed sexuality in a negative light. This obscured a healthy Christian attitude toward sex and may have damaged some people's growth. But today our society has gone to the other extreme and exalted sex for the sake of sex. We need to speak out and remind people of the dignity and value of sexual activity as a sign of committed love. Our world needs prophets who can brave ridicule and assert that sexual activity without the commitment of love is wrong. At the same time they must affirm that sexuality is a gift of God. Because sex comes from God, it is just as wrong to disdain the physical aspects of love as it is to promote loose sexual morality. The Sixth Commandment challenges us to root ourselves in love.

A scene in the film *Roots* charms the viewer as it depicts a girl discussing her emerging sexuality with her grandmother. When the child asks what these feelings are for, the grandmother replies: "Why child, for the joy, for the joy, that's what for." This response captures the Christian appreciation for sexuality. To use it in the proper moral context is to glorify God and grow in love for one's spouse. In this way God intends us to relish its delight.

For Personal Reflection

1. How do I understand my own sexuality? If I have questions or confusion in this part of life, how can I best resolve them?

2. Do I understand the Catholic Church's teaching on the richness of sexuality? Do I appreciate how this teaching can enhance my relationships?

3. Have I been or am I currently involved in activities or relationships which I know are damaging or sinful? What realistic steps can I take to change these?

4. In what ways do I need to pay more attention to the mystery of love and sexuality in my life?

Notes

Prayer

Lord Jesus,
you were fully divine and fully human—
like us in all things but sin.
Help me to understand
the mystery of my sexuality.
Free me from all the fear and hurt
that I may experience
in this complex part of life.
Fill me with a deep reverence for myself
and for others so that my desires and actions
will help me pay attention to love.
Make me brave in the face
of society's challenges and help me to stand
gently but firmly for the virtues
you have taught through your Church.
If I fail in right sexual conduct,
help me to turn immediately
to your merciful love and try again.

Amen.

Christian Honesty

We often think of honesty in narrow terms. We may think it means only to tell the truth and not steal. The Old Testament portrays some ideas about honesty which will enrich our understanding and challenge us to see how honest we really are. The Old Testament speaks of the *emeth Yahweh.* The word *emeth* is often translated as *truth.* The expression "God's truth" is a familiar expression. But *emeth* is a concept which embraces much more than that. It refers to God's fidelity. Ancient Israel saw the quality in God which made him always be as he should be. The God of Israel revealed that he is a God who is always ready to save his people through his constant, abiding presence. When the Seventh Commandment forbids dishonesty in all its forms, it is calling us to imitate the *emeth* of God. As God is faithful to his role as saving presence, we are asked to be faithful to the self he has created us to be.

Frequently we slip away from this sense of fidelity. We may attach more significance to not telling lies, returning the extra change at the store or not helping ourselves to the office supplies. While this is certainly part of honesty, it is only the beginning. Too often we settle for honest *actions* instead of forging honest *selves*. We work on frank *personalities* instead of whole and integrated *characters*. Honest people are free to be the persons whom God created them to be.

Many of our sins against honesty and truth flow out of a deficient sense of self. I may think that I simply must have this or that trinket to have status, so I pilfer until I have enough money to get that all-important key to acceptance. I may think that students who get high marks are superior to those with low grades, so I cheat on tests to clinch a coveted spot on the honor roll. At work I may cut corners to boost my job performance rating. If I meet an old friend, I may embellish descriptions of my job or family accomplishments so as to make a greater impression. In all these examples, my deficient sense of self goads me into being dishonest. To stop lying and cheating is only the beginning of living out the demands of the Seventh Commandment. The key to honest living is to appreciate and prize the self God has created in creating me, so that I will be able to let it shine forth. Then falsehood will evaporate like morning dew on the grass.

In his First Letter to the Corinthians, St. Paul writes: "By the grace of God I am what I am and his grace toward me was not in vain" (1 Cor 15:10). Paul was secure about his identity in Christ. Paul knew who he was, and he was able to be that person. He radiated honesty. He was able to be faithful to himself in imitation of the Christ he served. "For the Son of God, Jesus Christ, whom we preached among you, Silvanus and Timothy and I, is not yes and no; but in him it is always yes" (2 Cor 1:19).

The virtues of honesty and truth sparkle like the facets of a diamond. They do not merely prohibit falsehood. Instead, they involve a way of looking at the world, a way of being present to life which some philosophers and psychologists call an "intentionality." One dimension of this is a healthy sense of self which can embrace the world as it is, while laboring to transform it to what it ought to be. While the Seventh Commandment forbids dishonesty and falsehood, it also calls us to be people who are at home with ourselves. Such fearlessness fosters a resolve to hone and shape our world so that we can prepare for the coming of the kingdom of our God and of his Christ.

For Personal Reflection

1. Do I genuinelv know my true self and consistently portray that to others?

2. Do I engage in actions which I know to be dishonest? What is the underlying reason for those actions?

3. In what specific ways do I feel God calling me to greater fidelity to myself and his plan for me?

4. Do I understand the difference between personality and character? In what ways can I develop my character more deeply according to Christ's example and teaching?

Notes

Prayer

Lord Jesus Christ,
you are the source of all right judgments
and actions. Help me to develop a spirit
of honesty which grows out of a character
rooted in your example and the teaching
of your Gospel.
May I never say or do anything
which is contrary to the knowledge of myself
which your grace gives to me.
Make my work honest
and my relationships sincere.
Fill my life with the integrity that alone
comes from you who are Lord
forever and ever.

Amen.

Telling the Truth in Love

St. Paul characterizes the Christian life as "faith working through love" (Gal 5:6). If we rephrase Paul's description to "telling the truth in love," we gain an insight into what the Eighth Commandment means for us. This commandment prohibits all falsehood but especially that which tears down another's character or reputation. Obedience to the Eighth Commandment, however, goes beyond not telling lies. It demands that we speak the truth in love.

Most of us grew up with the cliché: "Honesty is the best policy." Whatever the truth of that adage, it doesn't express the fullness of what Christian love calls us to. For the Christian, honesty is not the primary virtue; love is. Love is the capstone of the virtues. While genuine love presumes honesty, it also requires that the truth be told in ways that are appropriate and respectful of persons and situations. A simple example might prove helpful. Suppose we have an obnoxious friend whom we would like to encourage to be less overbearing. As Christians we seek ways to speak the truth about that person's character in a gentle yet firm way. If we fail at this, we not only violate the spirit of the Eighth Commandment and the Gospel norm of charity, but will lose the opportunity for encouraging growth. Our obligation is not simply to tell the truth but to speak that truth in love.

Another trap which often ensnares us is the scourge of gossip. Every one of us has engaged in conversations which centered on another person's situation or character. While this might not be the most virtuous of pastimes, it differs from the gossip which the Eighth Commandment and Gospel charity prohibit. Gossip is the almost obsessive need to discuss and denigrate the character of others. As such, it always undermines the Christian community and undercuts our faithfulness to the Gospel. It is a disease which saps the strength from our commitment to God and his covenant, like a worm which gnaws out the heart of a tree. This is a strong indictment. But to eradicate this sinful reality from our lives we must name it for what it is and ask God for the strength to resist it whenever it tempts us.We may mask this destructive reality by dubbing it "the latest," "news" or "dirt." Every one of us enjoys having inside information. But when this involves belittling another or circulating half-truths or blatant lies, we flout God's covenant as expressed in the Gospel of his Son. Every member of the Christian community ought to challenge and confront gossip whenever it threatens to smear another person.

Why is it that telling the truth in love can be so difficult while falsehood and duplicity can slip into our conversation so easily? Perhaps it reflects a lack of confidence in ourselves as children of a loving God. St. Paul urges us: "Stand, therefore, having girded your loins with truth, and having put on the breastplate of righteousness, and having shod your feet with the equipment of the gospel of peace" (Eph 6:14-15). If we follow his advice, our conversations will reflect the law of love. They will serve to upbuild and enrich. When we are secure in who we are in Christ, we have no need to tear down someone else. When we recognize our own strengths and God-given talents, we can rejoice in the talents and accomplishments of others. When we acknowledge our own sinfulness, we can regard the faults of others with a compassionate eye.

By the grace of the covenant, God has made us custodians of truth. The Eighth Commandment insures that we will exercise this custody of the truth in a way that encourages and builds up the body of Christ. Our reflections on this commandment should stir us to pray for a courageous steadfastness which enables us to serve the truth which expresses itself in love.

For Personal Reflection

1. What are some specific instances in which I know I must tell the truth in love? How am I responding to these situations?

2. Am I sensitive to the way I speak the truth to others or do I sometimes use the truth as a "weapon"?

3. Are there occasions or habits of gossip in my life? What concrete ways can I use to eliminate them?

4. If my gossip has damaged someone's reputation, what specific things can I do to restore that person's good name?

Notes

Prayer

Lord Jesus Christ,
in you I find the perfection
of compassion and truth.
Deepen my love for the truth
and teach me forthright but
compassionate ways to proclaim it to all
whose lives I touch.
Give me the wisdom and integrity
to avoid gossip in all its forms.
May my thoughts and speech serve always
to build up rather than tear down,
to encourage rather than dishearten.
Make my life a humble but clear example
of telling the truth in love.

Amen.

We are Mysteries, Not Possessions

An old Shaker wedding song evokes the mystery of Christian marriage: "I'm in love with my God; my God is in love with me; and the more I love you the more I know that I'm in love with my God." In the wonder of Christian marriage God takes the love of two human beings and consecrates it into a sacrament—a sign of his love for us. The spirituality of marriage rests in the reality that as husband and wife fall more deeply in love with each other, they deepen their union with God. The Ninth Commandment is a precept which guarantees marital fidelity. It also challenges us to widen our concept of what Christian fidelity entails.

Human beings are essentially mysteries. Every one of us is made in the image and likeness of God, so we share in the utter incomprehensibility of God. Just as we shall never fully plumb the depths of his divinity, so we will always discover new and more profound insights into ourselves. The gift of fidelity in marriage is a lifelong opportunity to explore the riches found in another's personality. Fidelity enables me to recognize the mystery of others, particularly of my spouse. When we love another in the deepest Christian sense, we commit ourselves to living with their personal mystery. We can never own a mystery. But we can savor and appreciate it as the depth of its meaning gradually unfolds. Fidelity leads us into this realm of wonder. A child who peers into a kaleidoscope is amazed at the play of colors as they dance and dazzle the eye. But to peer into the depths of a person is to astonish one even more. The commitment of Christian marriage is to live with the mystery of my spouse. It is not a commitment to rule my spouse but a commitment to love, honor and cherish the mystery of this person given to me by God.

This dimension of marriage appeals to us. But the shadow side of human nature is apt to splatter the picture. Three pitfalls to be wary of are the need for novelty, the trap of the spouse/pet, and jealousy.

The world incites us to seek new thrills. We constantly search for novelty: we would like to drive a new sports car, wear the latest fashions, eat at the classiest new restaurants and see the most recent films. In a world which so allures us, a commitment to one person can seem to constrict us. Fidelity to my spouse doesn't thrive on novelty. It flourishes on a committment which can gaze into the core of that person and fathom the beauty there. The newness and change in marriage flows out of an ever-deeper understanding of this person with whom I share my years. We love one another with our virtues and sins, our nobility and our pettiness.

One of the greatest privileges of my priesthood has been to assist at the renewal of marriage vows of couples married twenty-five and fifty years. None of them said their marriage was perfect. Some had even suffered through tremendous pain in their relationship. But they all said that love surmounted the need for perfection, and understanding and commitment triumphed over all obstacles. Such is the fidelity which this commandment demands.

The second practical obstacle to living in marital fidelity is the trap of the spouse/pet. I know a man who raises pedigree dogs. He invests a great deal of time and money in this hobby. He grooms, shows, guards and cares for his German shepherds and golden retrievers with tremendous devotion. Very often we can treat those we love as if they are pets which we show off to amaze others. I might brag about my husband's new job or my wife's writing ability in order to impress friends and neighbors. But to value a spouse's accomplishments over who he or she is, invites tragedy. The Ninth Commandment prohibits any attitude which would detract from the respect I owe my spouse as a God-given mystery. Fidelity reveals the mystery hidden in his or her depths. I might lead my dog around on a leash, or display a trophy in a showcase, but I can't do that with the mystery of another person. Mysteries demand the surrender of ourselves. No one can surrender the deepest part of one's person to a pet. Only a cherished equal can bear the weight of such surrender.

In act three of Shakespeare's *Othello,* Iago warns against a fatal obstacle to happiness in marriage: "O, beware, my lord, of jealousy! It is the green-eyed monster, which doth mock the meat it feeds on." Many of us deny that we are jealous, since it betrays a certain immaturity. So we disguise it as concern or interest instead of admitting that the prospect of losing our loved one terrifies us. Any change in the beloved's status at work, school or in the community alarms us. We fear that someone else may beguile our loved one away from us. Jealousy poisons human relationships and breeds mistrust. It suspects that innocent friendships are dangerous liaisons. But when hearts are bound together in real love, the betterment of the other causes only joy. Love knows that when I share and rejoice in another's growth, I deepen my own mystery. A jealous heart leads one to be like the neighbor who peers out the window to keep track of the people across the street. Love instead thrives on openness and trust which celebrates the growth of my beloved.

Like many of life's great endeavors, marriage is more a process than an end. The points of this meditation are ideals to strive for more than goals to attain. If at times they may overwhelm us, this insight of T. S. Eliot can inspire us: "For us there is only the trying. The rest is not our business." The Ninth Commandment challenges us to love our spouse beyond possessiveness into the exciting precincts of mystery. We will often falter and grope our way in these uncharted passages. But in his infinite love and mercy, God understands our falls and blesses all our efforts.

I would like to end this reflection on a personal note. Some years ago a particularly painful disease struck my father. As he approached the point of death, my mother and sisters nursed him at home. At a certain point I feared that my mother was exhausting herself with work and stress, so I suggested that the time to hospitalize my father had arrived. She eyed me with determination. Fatigue and worry could not dampen the love that glowed in her face as she declared, "I married him in sickness and in health. I have had forty-two years of health and happiness. This is part of marriage, too. When it gets to be too much, I'll let you know." When we understand the kind of fidelity implied in my mother's words, the deepest meaning of the Ninth Commandment will be indelibly etched upon our hearts.

For Personal Reflection

1. Am I able to appreciate the "mystery" of my spouse? Is it time to recommit myself to this?

2. Do I ever experience jealousy in my marriage? How can I deal with these feelings in more Christ-like ways?

3. In what ways do I try to possess or own my spouse or others whom I say I love? What specific means can I use to change this?

4. Do I strive to be faithful when my marriage becomes difficult, or have I developed clever means of "running away"?

Notes

Prayer

Lord Jesus Christ,
you graced the wedding feast at Cana
with your miraculous power. Help me
to appreciate the miracle of my own marriage.
Deepen the love and trust of my spouse
and myself.
In difficulty and in joy may we always respect
the mystery of each other and the even deeper
mystery of your presence in our marriage.
May we never hide from our difficulties
but seek to live in realistic fidelity
to the vows we have made.
When we fail in love for each other, bring us
your healing and the grace to try again.
We ask the same healing for all couples
who are in difficulty.
For those whose marriages have ended we ask
a special grace of comfort and peace. As we
live our married life, help us to believe ever
more firmly that the more we love each other,
the closer we grow to you,
the Father and the Holy Spirit,
who live and reign as one God
forever and ever.

Amen.

Being and Having

I have observed a phenomenon among college students which should be distressing to Christians. It is becoming more and more difficult to find a young person who will major in anything but the business fields. While there is certainly nothing wrong or unchristian about a career in business, this points to a disturbing reality. When asked why they are pursuing a higher education, many students will respond: "To get a job." Their majors indicate that they seek highly-paid business positions. These students have forgotten that the purpose of higher education is not to make a living but to make a life worth living. Like many of us, they seek financial security and material possessions. Fewer students pursue professions which may earn less money but will enrich them with opportunities for service.

The Tenth Commandment prohibits coveting another's possessions and cautions against avarice. The Christian philosopher Gabriel Marcel stressed *being* over *having;* that who we are is more important than what we possess or the skills we acquire. We are more valuable for who we are than for what we have or what we can do. The Tenth Commandment invites us to realize that our being is more significant than the things we own.

Money and possessions are not sinful in themselves. But how much of ourselves do we surrender to acquire them? When we covet someone else's Mercedes or beach house, we overlook that we are valuable for who we are, not what we possess. Advertising feeds off this desire to possess. It creates needs and then lures us into buying what we crave. The Tenth Commandment reminds us that only God can satisfy our longings. As St. Augustine exclaimed in his *Confessions:* "You made us for yourself, O Lord, and our hearts are restless until they rest in you."

In Robert Bolt's play *A Man for all Seasons,* Thomas More encounters the avaricious Richard Rich. Through dishonesty and manipulation, Rich has maneuvered himself into being appointed the attorney general for Wales. Trapped in his own web of deceit, Rich then purjures himself during More's trial. More reproaches him: "Why, Richard, it profits a man nothing to give his soul for the whole world...but for Wales!" How many of us trade our integrity for a bauble, a position, security or recognition? The Master's hand molded us with infinite love and we disregard the beauty God has breathed into us.

The Tenth Commandment invites us to consider how we value ourselves. It challenges us to unmask the motives for our actions. Why do I go out to buy the shirt my friend was wearing when my closet bulges with clothes? How many VCRs do I need? Do I vacation so that I can relax and enjoy my family, or do I go on a Caribbean cruise just to boast about it? It is not a vice to have comfortable things or to desire the best for my family. But do I compromise myself to acquire things which ultimately leave me empty?

The last commandment of the decalogue forbids us to exchange our honesty for any possession. It invites us to focus our vision on who we are. When we can rest securely in our identity in Christ, we will not covet our neighbor's possessions or let advertising allure us.

Jesus could be very direct when he had to be. In the sixteenth chapter of Matthew's Gospel, we find him posing the question to his disciples: "What does it profit a man if he gain the whole world and suffer the loss of himself?" That question haunts each one of us in the silence of our hearts. How we answer it will determine if we value *being* over *having* in our lives. How we answer it will determine who—or what—is the real Lord of our lives.

For Personal Reflection

1. Do I believe that I am more important for who I am than for what I possess, or have I become more materialistic than I might wish to recognize?

2. In my life, how much is enough?

3. Are there ways in which my possessions have come to own me, decreasing my ability or my desire to give God first place in my life?

4. In what specific ways can I deepen the realization that only God can fulfill the deepest longings of my heart?

Notes

Prayer

Lord God,
you are the Creator of all things.
Help me to seek you in all aspects of my life.
May my appreciation and desire for
the beauty of your creation never blind me
to my real desire for you, the Creator.
Never allow me to surrender myself
for earthly possessions
but deepen my understanding
that you have made me for yourself
and my heart will always be restless
until it rests in you.

Amen.

Afterword

"And behold, one came up to him, saying, 'Teacher, what good deed must I do, to have eternal life?' And he said to him, 'Why do you ask me about what is good? One there is who is good. If you would enter life, keep the commandments.' He said to him, 'Which?' And Jesus said, 'You shall not kill, You shall not commit adultery, You shall not steal, You shall not bear false witness, Honor your father and mother, and, You shall love your neighbor as yourself.' The young man said to him, 'All these I have observed; what do I still lack?' Jesus said to him, 'If you would be perfect, go, sell what you possess and give to the poor, and you will have treasure in heaven; and come, follow me.' When the young man heard this he went away sorrowful; for he had great possessions" (Mt 19:16-22).

This Gospel account saddens and challenges us. It saddens us to see the young man refuse Christ's invitation to a more profound union with God. It challenges us to break the bonds that chain us to possessions. Then our hearts can fly to the Lord, like the eagle which soars into the sky. The Ten Commandments point out the way to God. They are means to that goal. As we come to the end of our meditations, we find that they have led us to Jesus, and we can hear his invitation: "Come follow me." These meditations are valuable only to the extent that they enable us to respond to that call and follow Christ more closely. For the Christian, the great goal is Christ. "I press on toward the goal for the prize of the upward call of God in Christ Jesus" (Phil 3:14).

Too often we become slavish followers of a spirituality, a movement or a particular spiritual guide or director. But only one figure commands our allegiance: the crucified and risen Lord, who came that we might have life and have it more abundantly. Any program of spiritual growth must begin in Jesus Christ, be sustained and supported by him, and end in him. This truth is the foundation of all spirituality. To alter it in any way is to rob the Lord of the centrality he must have in our hearts. "None of us lives to himself, and none of us dies to himself. If we live, we live to the Lord; and if we die, we die to the Lord; so then, whether we live or die we are the Lord's" (Rom 14:7-8). TheTen Commandments lead us to belong more fully to the Lord, both in what they explicitly prohibit and in what they implicitly demand.

Words like "call," "invitation" and "challenge" appear frequently in these meditations. They indicate that God draws us to union with himself with delicacy and tender respect for our frail human nature. But these thoughts would be radically incomplete if they did not focus also on the imperatives of the decalogue. In May 1987, TV personality Ted Koppel gave the commencement address at Duke University. During that talk he observed: "What Moses brought down from Mount Sinai were not the Ten Suggestions. They are commandments. *Are,* not *were*. The sheer brilliance of the Ten Commandments is that they codify in a handful of words acceptable human behavior, not just for then or now, but for all time."

Both in what they forbid and what they demand, the Ten Commandments flood our path with light as we journey toward God. Unyielding in their demands and radical in their scope, they push Christians beyond the niceties of religious observance. They thrust us into what we might otherwise fear to plunge into: the adventure of a life totally given over to the absolute demands of following Christ.

Jesus once issued an absolute and radical call to a young man. The youth went away sad because his attachment to possessions blinded him from seeing beyond the letter of the law to its spirit. So he refused Jesus' invitation. Had he accepted, grace would have enabled him to follow Christ. The preceding reflections were meant to spur us to fervor on the days when zeal fires us, prod us to action on the days when fatigue saps us, and to hearten us on the days when troubles worry us. These keys will unlock the treasures of silent, prayerful encounters with the Lord. His grace alone will insure that, unlike the young man of the Gospel, we may never go away sad.

Pauline BOOKS & MEDIA

ALASKA
750 West 5th Ave., Anchorage, AK 99501; 907-272-8183

CALIFORNIA
3908 Sepulveda Blvd., Culver City, CA 90230; 310-397-8676
5945 Balboa Ave., San Diego, CA 92111; 619-565-9181
46 Geary Street, San Francisco, CA 94108; 415-781-5180

FLORIDA
145 S.W. 107th Ave., Miami, FL 33174; 305-559-6715

HAWAII
1143 Bishop Street, Honolulu, HI 96813; 808-521-2731

ILLINOIS
172 North Michigan Ave., Chicago, IL 60601; 312-346-4228

LOUISIANA
4403 Veterans Memorial Blvd., Metairie, LA 70006; 504-887-7631

MASSACHUSETTS
50 St. Paul's Ave., Jamaica Plain, Boston, MA 02130; 617-522-8911
Rte. 1, 885 Providence Hwy., Dedham, MA 02026; 617-326-5385

MISSOURI
9804 Watson Rd., St. Louis, MO 63126; 314-965-3512

NEW JERSEY
561 U.S. Route 1, Wick Plaza, Edison, NJ 08817; 908-572-1200

NEW YORK
150 East 52nd Street, New York, NY 10022; 212-754-1110
78 Fort Place, Staten Island, NY 10301; 718-447-5071

OHIO
2105 Ontario Street, Cleveland, OH 44115; 216-621-9427

PENNSYLVANIA
Northeast Shopping Center, 9171-A Roosevelt Blvd. (between Grant Ave. & Welsh Rd.), Philadelphia, PA 19114; 215-676-9494

SOUTH CAROLINA
243 King Street, Charleston, SC 29401; 803-577-0175

TENNESSEE
4811 Poplar Ave., Memphis, TN 38117; 901-761-2987

TEXAS
114 Main Plaza, San Antonio, TX 78205; 210-224-8101

VIRGINIA
1025 King Street, Alexandria, VA 22314; 703-549-3806

CANADA
3022 Dufferin Street, Toronto, Ontario, Canada M6B 3T5; 416-781-9131